DEVELOPMENTAL ASSIGNMENTS

Creating Learning Experiences without Changing Jobs

Center for Creative Leadership

NORTH AMERICA EUROPE ASIA

www.ccl.org

The Center for Creative Leadership is an international, nonprofit educational institution founded in 1970 to advance the understanding, practice, and development of leadership for the benefit of society worldwide. As a part of this mission, it publishes books and reports that aim to contribute to a general process of inquiry and understanding in which ideas related to leadership are raised, exchanged, and evaluated. The ideas presented in its publications are those of the author or authors.

The Center thanks you for supporting its work through the purchase of this volume. If you have comments, suggestions, or questions about any CCL Press publication, please contact the Director of Publications at the address given below.

Center for Creative Leadership
Post Office Box 26300
Greensboro, North Carolina 27438-6300
Telephone 336 288 7210
www.ccl.org

Cynthia D. McCauley

DEVELOPMENTAL ASSIGNMENTS

Creating Learning Experiences without Changing Jobs

CENTER FOR CREATIVE LEADERSHIP
Greensboro, North Carolina

CCL Stock No. 189
©2006 Center for Creative Leadership

Published by CCL Press
Martin Wilcox, Director of Publications
Peter Scisco, Editor, CCL Press
Karen Mayworth, Associate Editor
Joanne Ferguson, Production Editor

Cover design by Joanne Ferguson

Library of Congress Cataloging-in-Publication Data

McCauley, Cynthia D. (Cynthia Denise), 1958–
    Developmental assignments : creating learning experiences without changing jobs / Cynthia D. McCauley.
        p. cm. — (CCL ; stock no. 189)
    Includes bibliographical references.
    ISBN-10: 1-882197-91-7 [ISBN-13: 978-1-882197-91-0]
    1. Executive ability—Handbooks, manuals, etc. 2. Career development—Handbooks, manuals, etc. 3. Needs assessment—Handbooks, manuals, etc. 4. Leadership—Handbooks, manuals, etc. I. Title. II. Series: Report (Center for Creative Leadership) ; no. 189.

    HD38.2.M3932 2006
    658.4'07124—dc22

                                                    2005033642

CONTENTS

ACKNOWLEDGMENTS

This fieldbook is based on a stream of research and application on learning from job assignments that involved numerous colleagues over many years. In particular, I have drawn heavily from the work of Kerry Bunker, Maxine Dalton, Bob Eichinger, George Hollenbeck, Mike Lombardo, Morgan McCall, Patty Ohlott, and Marian Ruderman. More recent conversations with Ed Betoff, Bill Howland, Sharon Lamm, Stephanie Lischke, and Joe Toto about their use of the Job Challenge Profile also sparked ideas for the book. Thanks go to Pete Scisco and Kelly Lombardino for their encouragement to undertake this endeavor. Finally, I am grateful to Stephanie Lischke, Steve McMillen, Clare Norman, and Joe Toto for their careful review and feedback on earlier drafts of the book.

INTRODUCTION

The purpose of this fieldbook is to help you as a leader more intentionally seek out and design your own developmental assignments (and to help others do the same). It focuses in particular on how to shape your current job and nonwork pursuits so that these activities will provide opportunities to continuously stretch and grow as a leader. We often refer to this approach to learning as development in place because it doesn't require a major job shift or a move to a new organization. It often does, however, require working with your boss or with others inside or outside the organization to add responsibilities to your job or engage in temporary tasks or roles. We refer to these responsibilities and tasks as assignments. They become developmental assignments when they serve as a source of learning and growth.

This fieldbook is modeled after *Eighty-Eight Assignments for Development in Place* (Lombardo & Eichinger, 1989), one of CCL's most popular publications. In the years since that report was published, we have learned more about development in place—from research, from working with managers and organizations who are making use of developmental assignments, and from our colleagues in the field. Our frameworks for describing job challenges and the competencies managers develop from facing those challenges have evolved. Thus, we believe it is time once again to consolidate our knowledge into one tool to help people add developmental assignments to their current jobs.

This fieldbook is organized as follows:

- Background: Chapter 1 provides the rationale for seeking a wide variety of developmental assignments during your career. It provides descriptions from leaders of their own development-in-place experiences. And it defines ten major job challenges that drive on-the-job learning.

- Development in Place: Chapter 2 provides a step-by-step process for choosing a developmental assignment. You will see that there are various options and choices to be made along the way. The chapter concludes with strategies for maximizing learning from assignments.

- Assignments: Chapters 3 and 4 contain tables that are full of examples of development-in-place assignments. The tables will help you target examples that will best fit your learning and development needs. You might find an assignment listed that you hadn't thought of as an option. And the examples will likely spark additional ideas for assignments— ones that are highly specific to your organization or situation. The tables are by no means exhaustive; they are intended to help you generate new possibilities.

- Appendixes: Here you will find resources, a template you can use to create your own developmental assignment plan, and cross-references to CCL's assessment tools: 360 by Design, Executive Dimensions, Benchmarks, Prospector, and Skillscope. If you want to target the development of specific competencies as a result of receiving feedback from one of CCL's assessments, these cross-references will direct you to appropriate assignments based on that feedback. The appendix lists the specific competencies for the assessment tool, along with page numbers for related assignments.

1

BACKGROUND

Research and practice at the Center for Creative Leadership strongly support three key conclusions about leader development:

- **Effective leaders continue to develop their repertoire of skills throughout their careers.** Most leaders begin their careers with clear strengths that they bring to their work. These strengths vary from leader to leader; possibilities include ease at building productive relationships, the ability to synthesize and create order out of a large amount of information, and resiliency in the face of adversity. But to be effective in a wide variety of leadership roles and situations, individuals have to master new skills and develop proficiency in additional arenas. Instead of always relying on a limited set of natural capabilities, they have to become more well-rounded. This development of a repertoire of skills is a gradual, continuous process—although there may be periods when leaders experience a sense of more rapid learning. It is also important to remember that no single leader becomes adept at all the myriad skills that can be applied to leadership work. The important point is that effective leaders—whatever their beginning base of strength—work to broaden their repertoire.

- **A significant part of this development occurs through practical experiences.** Effective leaders who have been on this journey report work and life experiences as a rich source of their ongoing learning and growth. This is consistent with what we know about adult learning. Adults learn when their day-to-day responsibilities and challenges require it—

and when they have the opportunity to engage in experiences, draw lessons and insights from those experiences, and apply this new knowledge and skills to the next experience. Leaders also learn from formal training and development activities and through their relationships, but "learning by doing" is a central process in leader development.

- **The more varied the practical experiences, the greater the likelihood of developing a broad repertoire of skills.** Leaders who continue to focus only on doing the work that they are already good at are less likely to broaden their leadership capacity. Leaders who step into new situations and face challenges that call for untested abilities continue to develop their capacity and successfully take on higher levels of leadership responsibility. Certainly, these leaders apply their strengths to their "stretch" experiences, but they also are aware that these experiences ignite their "growing edge," where deeper knowledge is discovered and new capabilities are honed.

These conclusions lead to the advice we give to leaders about their own development: shape your work and life experiences so that they will provide the opportunities to expand your leadership knowledge and skills. As you will see in the descriptions that follow, the paths to these practical learning experiences are varied.

Descriptions of Development in Place

Sometimes developmental assignments are thrust upon people, as in these examples from two leaders:

I was a manager in an accounting firm, and a large commercial bank was about to terminate us because of poor service. I was assigned to save the office's largest client. This difficult challenge required selecting the right staff, negotiating the services with the client, and ensuring top-quality work. The end result was that the bank stayed and we were able to receive significant add-on services. I learned what great teamwork takes—including making the customer part of the team.

While assigned as an industrial engineer at my first overseas post, I was given a special assignment in production control to improve the effectiveness of production scheduling. I possessed no previous experience in scheduling, had to deal in a foreign language that I was just learning, and was trying to figure out what *scheduling* meant in a culture that did not value speed and efficiency in ways that I did. I gained a lot of confidence from this experience. I realized that I could learn the language and the techniques of a whole new area quickly and make a contribution.

At other times, people choose to pursue a task or activity that's not a normal part of their work primarily because the activity has potential value for the organization (or some larger cause). They expect the experience to be developmental, but they haven't chosen the activity for that reason. As can be seen in the next two examples, these assignments can be inside or outside the work setting.

I saw a great new business opportunity for my division and pursued it. It involved extensive strategic and financial analysis, formal recommendation to corporate, acquisition of a small company, and integration into our division. The outcome was good for the organization and for me. I learned to integrate a great deal of data, improved my negotiation skills, and impressed my boss enough to get a promotion.

I went with a church group to Mexico to build an addition to a small school. I didn't know any of the people on the team. We had to quickly learn how to work together. Some of us had more building expertise than others, but we discovered that everyone had a strength to contribute to the work. This was important because it was hard work! I learned about the power of a unifying set of values for motivating diverse people to contribute to a team.

And finally, individuals also pursue developmental assignments intentionally, either because their current jobs aren't providing enough development or they are targeting a particular development need.

One of my colleagues and I were grumbling about the fact that we felt we were getting stale in our jobs. We hit upon the idea of trading off a couple of our projects. She was in marketing research, and I was in public relations. We sold this to our bosses as on-the-job development. We both learned about a function we had little exposure to. One mistake we made was not selling this switch to the other people on the projects. I encountered some subtle resistance that took me a while to pick up on. But the project team and I ended up having a straightforward conversation. I learned that they thought this project was just a "playground" for me. I reassured them and continued demonstrating my commitment to the work. I learned to put myself in other people's shoes and see how things must look from their perspective.

My boss and I agreed that I tend to shy away from problems that require a lot of cross-functional input and have political ramifications. As part of my development plan, he put me in charge of investigating and bringing back recommendations about the potential outsourcing of three business services. This forced me to work with some other functions in a politically charged atmosphere—although my boss continued to support and coach me throughout. I learned that if you provide enough useful information and set the right tone, people can make good decisions that balance multiple criteria.

What these examples have in common is that the developmental assignment did not require taking on a whole new job. And the assignment challenged the individuals, stretching them beyond their current skills. Challenge is one of the key elements of a developmental assignment. But the examples also highlight the wide variety of challenges a leader might face in an assignment. What might be the right challenge for you as you continue to expand your repertoire of leadership skills? The job challenge framework can help you start to answer that question.

Job Challenges

The job challenge framework helps individuals identify developmental assignments. It is based on a series of research projects on managerial learning, growth, and change. These studies clearly pointed to the central role played by job assignments in the development of successful leaders. The research identifies a number of key challenges—characteristics or features of assignments that stimulate learning:

- Unfamiliar responsibilities—handling responsibilities that are new or very different from previous ones you've handled

- New directions—starting something new or making strategic changes

- Inherited problems—fixing problems created by someone else or existing before you took the assignment

- Problems with employees—dealing with employees who lack adequate experience, are incompetent, or are resistant to change

- High stakes—managing work with tight deadlines, pressure from above, high visibility, and responsibility for critical decisions
- Scope and scale—managing work that is broad in scope (involving multiple functions, groups, locations, products, or services) or large in sheer size (for example, workload, number of responsibilities)
- External pressure—managing the interface with important groups outside the organization, such as customers, vendors, partners, unions, and regulatory agencies
- Influence without authority—influencing peers, higher management, or other key people over whom you have no authority
- Work across cultures—working with people from different cultures or with institutions in other countries
- Work group diversity—being responsible for the work of people of both genders and different racial and ethnic backgrounds

The research also points to another key dynamic of continuous learning: to continue to develop their repertoire of skills, leaders need to be constantly seeking out these types of challenges. As we worked with leaders who were trying to be more intentional about their development, a more systematic approach—development in place—emerged.

2
DEVELOPMENT IN PLACE

When you think about seeking out new challenges, the first thing that likely comes to mind is getting a new job—usually one that gives you broader responsibilities and moves you up the hierarchy. Or you may think of a move into a different business unit or function to gain knowledge and practical experience in an important part of the organization. You may even think of moving to a new organization to broaden your industry experience.

Certainly these major job shifts are often the most developmental experiences in a career. You will likely take on new responsibilities, carry out different tasks, and interact with a whole new set of people. Major job moves are also important as you think about advancing your career. The problem from a developmental perspective with thinking only about these types of moves is that they are infrequent, you face lots of competition for them (particularly the higher up you go in the organization), and you don't have very much control over whether you get them. For learning and development to be ongoing and for it to be more under your control, seeking out new challenges in the context of your current job is a practical strategy to pursue.

There are two basic approaches to development in place:

- **Add challenges that will broaden your experience base.** Look back at the ten key challenges listed previously. Remember that these key challenges provide experience-based learning opportunities. You should seek to experience each of these challenges multiple times during the course of your career. To pick a challenge to add to your current work, ask yourself questions like these: Which of the challenges have I had the least exposure to? Are there some that I haven't experienced in a number of years? Are there any that my current job never provides?

- **Add challenges that target the development of a particular competency.** Right now you may be trying to improve a particular leadership capability (for example, communication skills, adaptability, or strategic thinking). Or there may be one you've wanted to work on but just haven't had the opportunity. A key way to develop a targeted capability is to practice it in real-life settings. It is hard to develop new communication skills if you are never in situations that call for these skills. It's hard to become a more competent strategic thinker if your job calls for you to focus only on the day-to-day. Developmental assignments can be targeted to provide the kind of experiences you need to practice and improve a particular skill.

Adding Developmental Assignments

There are several ways to add developmental assignments to your current job. One approach is reshaping your job. Basically this means adding new responsibilities to your job on a more or less permanent basis. These new responsibilities might be moved from someone else's plate to your own. They might be tasks that need to be done but that no one is currently "owning." Or they could be responsibilities that are already a legitimate part of your job, but you've tended to pay little attention to them—maybe because they seemed like something you wouldn't be good at!

Another way to seek developmental assignments is through temporary assignments. These are tasks or responsibilities that are bounded by time: projects, task forces, one-time events, activities you can participate in for a short period of time.

A final strategy is to seek challenges outside the workplace. There are plenty of leadership responsibilities that people take on outside their places of employment—in community, nonprofit, religious, social, and professional organizations, as well as in their families. These settings often have the same challenges found in job settings. As we have heard from many of the leaders we work with, there are many opportunities to learn lessons of leadership through personal life experiences.

Choosing Your Developmental Assignment

In chapters 3 and 4, you will find two sets of tables that will help you craft your own developmental assignments. The examples in these tables came from interviews with managers about their developmental assignments, from actual development plans that individuals have crafted, and from suggestions provided by leadership development consultants. There is much overlap in the examples given in the two sets of tables. They are the same examples for the most part, but organized in two different ways: by challenge and by competency.

Challenge-Driven Assignments. The tables in chapter 3 are designed to support the first approach to development in place described above: add challenges that will broaden your experience base. If you choose this approach, simply look through the ten key challenges and pick one that you want to add to your experience base. For each challenge, there's a table containing examples of how this challenge could be experienced by reshaping your job, adding a temporary assignment, or seeking a challenge outside the workplace. At the top of the table, you will also find a brief description of the challenge and the kind of learning opportunities it provides.

You might find an example in the table that fits your situation and that you can pursue. But you are just as likely to use these examples to stimulate your own ideas of how you could add a specific type of challenge. Because organizations vary a great deal in the kind of work they do, how they organize that work, and the systems and processes that support the work, it is difficult to provide examples that are relevant in all contexts. For example, some organizations frequently use task forces and cross-functional teams while others do not. There are many more opportunities to interface with customers in some organizations than in others. You may need to customize the examples or add new ones that fit your situation.

Competency-Driven Assignments. The tables in chapter 4 are designed to support the second approach to development in place: target the development of a specific skill. These tables are organized around CCL's Model of Leader Competencies, which delineates twenty competencies that support leader effectiveness. We use this model to illustrate the broad repertoire of knowledge, skills, and abilities that are useful to individuals when they are in leadership roles and take on leadership responsibilities. We also use it to help leaders identify competencies they need to develop further. The competencies are divided into three broad categories: Leading Yourself, Leading Others, and Leading the Organization.

If you choose the second approach, look through the twenty competencies and pick the one that is most similar to the competency you want to improve. The second column in each table describes in broad terms the types of assignments that could help you develop a particular competency and then provides specific examples of these assignments. As in the first set of tables, examples cover the three basic ways of adding developmental assignments to your job: reshaping your job, temporary assignments, and seeking challenge outside the workplace.

And as with the first set of tables, the examples are meant to stimulate your own ideas of how you can seek a targeted develop-

mental assignment. One thing to keep in mind when using the second approach: You develop a competency as you have the opportunity to practice the competency. So when generating your own ideas, ask yourself what responsibility you might add, what task you might take on, what you might get involved in that would force you to practice the competency. This question will also help you generate ideas if you have chosen to work on a competency that doesn't fit well with any of those in our model.

Guidelines. Whichever set of tables you choose to focus on, follow these guidelines:

- Don't just rely on yourself to generate specific ideas for your developmental assignment; share some of the examples with coworkers or friends and ask for their suggestions and their knowledge of what assignments might be doable or available.

- Narrow down your list of potential examples and discuss them with your boss: Which ones have the most promise in terms of both practicality and learning potential? Which ones would also be particularly beneficial to your group or to the organization? Who else will need to be brought into the conversation to make the assignment a reality? Leave the discussion with a game plan.

- Have both a short-term and long-term approach to developmental assignments. You might be able to orchestrate some developmental assignments rather quickly. You might have to keep others in the back of your mind, looking for the right opportunity to emerge. And for others, you may be able to lay some groundwork in order to better ensure that the opportunity will develop later.

Maximizing Learning from Assignments

Having a challenging assignment doesn't necessarily mean that you will learn a great deal from the assignment; that is, it doesn't guarantee that it will be a *developmental* assignment. You could face the challenge using the well-developed skills you already have in your repertoire, never giving yourself the opportunity to practice something new. You could bulldoze your way through the challenge, never stepping back to reflect on what you might be thinking, feeling, or learning. As you work your way through the assignment, you could gain some new insights that you tuck away, never to apply again in future work. Or you could maximize your learning and development throughout the assignment by engaging in multiple types of learning tactics:

Action. When individuals are using action tactics, they are learning by doing. They immerse themselves in the situation to figure things out. They work in a trial-and-error fashion, seeing what works and what doesn't. They do not wait until all the information is in before making a move. This tactic is essential in developmental assignments. Remember that you won't develop new skills if you aren't putting them into action during the assignment.

Thinking. When individuals are using thinking tactics, they are learning by reflecting and imagining. They compare the current challenge to past situations, looking for parallels, contrasts, and rules of thumb. They imagine how different options might play out. They mentally rehearse actions before engaging in them. And they regularly access articles, books, or the Internet to gain knowledge or information.

Feeling. When individuals are using feeling tactics, they are managing the anxiety and uncertainty associated with undertaking new challenges. They consider how they and others are feeling. They acknowledge the impact of these feelings on what they decide to do. They confront themselves when they recognize that their worry is causing them to avoid the challenge.

Accessing others. When individuals are using the tactic of accessing others, they seek advice, examples, support, feedback, or instruction from other people (particularly from those who have met a challenge similar to the one they face). They also look for role models and learn by watching others.

Crafting Your Developmental Assignment Plan

As you prepare for a developmental assignment, craft a plan that makes use of multiple types of learning tactics. Your development plan should address the following questions:

- What skills, behaviors, or actions do I need to practice in this assignment?

- How will I get feedback on how well I am applying these skills, behaviors, or actions?

- What experiences from my past can I draw on for potential use in this assignment?

- What formal body of knowledge do I need to access for potential use in this assignment?

- Whom should I access for advice on how to approach this assignment?

- What about this assignment produces the most anxiety for me? How will I make sure I don't avoid those aspects of the assignment?

- Who would be a good coach or role model for me during this assignment?

- Who will support and reenergize me when the assignment starts feeling like too much?

On the next page is an example of a developmental assignment plan that incorporates multiple learning tactics. (See Appendix B for a blank form to use for your own plan.)

Developmental Assignment Plan

Developmental Assignment: Investigate and provide recommendations on whether to outsource three business services currently operating in-house.

Time Frame: February to June

Target of Development: Ability to engage people from different functions in making politically charged decisions.

Skills, Behaviors, Actions to Practice:
- Separating fact from opinion or assumptions
- Facilitating discussions in which conflicting points of view are heard and respected

Resources to Access:
- Review best-practice studies on outsourcing.
- Interview individuals in the organization involved in past decisions about outsourcing.

Relationships to Put in Place:
- Get agreement with my boss to serve as a coach.
- Create a mechanism to get feedback from participants in the project on how well I am doing on the two skills listed above.
- Ask John D., a colleague, to serve as a sounding board during the assignment.

Other Strategies:
- Keep a journal to reflect on any anxiety I am experiencing and what I am learning.

Assessment and Support

In CCL's experience with leader development, we note that for an experience to be developmental, three elements need to be present: assessment, challenge, and support. As stated earlier, challenge is one of the key elements of a developmental assignment. It's what people should look for when seeking a developmental assignment. However, assessment and support need to be built into the assignment—they often aren't natural parts of the work. Assessment includes the formal and informal processes for getting data about how you are doing in the assignment. Feedback from others is a common source of assessment, although self-reflection and getting reactions from a coach also provide assessment data. Support helps you effectively deal with the struggles of a challenging assignment. Support usually comes from coworkers, but can also come from family and friends. Support is also communicated by the organization through showing general confidence in your ability to take on the assignment and giving you necessary resources.

Another way of thinking about a development plan is that it helps you—in a very systematic and intentional way—call out the challenge you will face in the developmental assignment and build strategies for getting the assessment and support you will need to maximize learning from the assignment.

3
CHALLENGE-DRIVEN ASSIGNMENTS

This chapter is designed to support development in place by adding challenges that will broaden your experience base. If you choose this approach, simply look through the ten key challenges and pick one that you want to add to your experience base. For each challenge, there's a table containing examples of how this challenge could be experienced by reshaping your job, adding a temporary assignment, or seeking a challenge outside the workplace. At the top of the table, you will also find a brief description of the challenge and the kind of learning opportunities it provides.

Unfamiliar Responsibilities

Description: Handling responsibilities that are new or very different from previous ones you've handled.

Benefits: Gives you the opportunity to practice new skills and expand your knowledge base. Also allows you to learn how to operate effectively when you are early in a learning curve.

Reshaping Your Job	Temporary Assignments	Outside the Workplace
Ask your boss to delegate one of his/her job responsibilities to you.	Take on part of a colleague's job while he/she is on temporary leave.	Volunteer for a task that you've never done before in a community or professional organization.
Take on a responsibility you had previously delegated to a more experienced subordinate.	Represent your group on a task force or committee doing work you know little about (e.g., examining a business issue or an emerging market).	Take up a new hobby.
Trade a responsibility with a colleague.		Trade a family responsibility with another family member (e.g., managing finances, hosting a family reunion, helping children with homework).
Add to your job a responsibility that is currently "falling through the cracks" in your group.	Volunteer for a task that would normally go to a more experienced person in your group.	
Focus more attention and effort on a part of your job you've been avoiding.	Participate in a job rotation program.	Go on an adventure (e.g., travel somewhere you haven't been, go to events you never attend, seek out people you don't normally meet).
	Design your own job rotation program: spend four to six weeks in three other units that interface with your own unit.	

New Directions

Description: Starting something new or making strategic changes.

Benefits: Gives you the opportunity to take initiative, explore and create, and organize people to make things happen. Also helps you to learn to operate in ambiguous situations and think strategically.

Reshaping Your Job	Temporary Assignments	Outside the Workplace
Be responsible for a new project or new process in your group. Develop five-year business scenarios for your unit. Develop new strategies for accomplishing some aspect of your work. • Reorganize a system in response to customer demands. • Work with colleagues to redesign a work process.	Join a project team that is plowing new ground in your organization (e.g., opening a new market, developing new products, installing new systems, opening new facilities, acquiring another company). Volunteer your work group as a test site for a new organizational system or process. Actively participate in the start-up of a new team. Start up something small. • Seek seed money for an exploratory project. • Design a workshop to help colleagues learn more about a "hot" topic. Work with your direct reports as a group to reorganize their work responsibilities to better fit with organizational priorities. Take a temporary assignment in the strategic planning or new product development function.	Work on a strategic plan for a community or professional organization. Start a new group, club, or team. Head a new initiative for a community or professional organization. Help facilitate the merger of two community or nonprofit organizations.

Inherited Problems

Description: Fixing problems created by someone else or existing before you took the assignment.

Benefits: Gives you the opportunity to tackle problems, diagnose and understand root causes, and reenergize people. Also helps you learn to make tough decisions and persevere in the face of adversity.

Reshaping Your Job	Temporary Assignments	Outside the Workplace
Take on the "fix it" role in your group or function.	Ask your group to give you one new problem a year to solve.	Join the board of a struggling nonprofit organization.
• Take on the most dissatisfied customers or difficult suppliers.	• Redesign a flawed product or system.	Work to improve your relationship with a difficult neighbor.
• Take over troubled projects.	• Correct quality problems.	
• Supervise product recalls.	• Streamline product development cycle time.	Advocate for a social or environmental cause.
• Supervise cost-cutting initiatives.	• Regain a lost customer.	
• Manage a continuous quality improvement process.	• Improve metrics used to assess effectiveness.	Lead a quality improvement initiative in a nonprofit or professional organization.
• Investigate outsourcing opportunities.	Serve on a task force to solve a major organizational problem.	
	Investigate and make a decision about whether to continue resourcing a project that continues to underperform.	

Problems with Employees

Description: Dealing with employees who lack adequate experience, are incompetent, or are resistant to change.

Benefits: Gives you the opportunity to deal with people problems, face and resolve conflict, and coach employees to higher levels of performance. Also provides an opportunity to learn to balance toughness and empathy.

Reshaping Your Job	Temporary Assignments	Outside the Workplace
Take on the responsibility of coaching employees with performance problems in your group.	Resolve a conflict with a subordinate.	Coach a sports team.
	Commit to handling an employee performance issue you've been avoiding.	Be trained as a volunteer mediator.
Manage the training of new employees in your group.	Hire and implement a development plan for an employee who shows promise but doesn't have the needed experience for the job.	
Delegate one of your job responsibilities to a direct report.	Work to retain a valued employee who is thinking about leaving the organization.	
	Fire an employee who has not met performance standards despite coaching and support.	
	Champion a change your group has been resisting (e.g., using a new organizational procedure or switching to a new technology).	
	Engage your direct reports in a goal alignment exercise.	

High Stakes

Description: Managing work with tight deadlines, pressure from above, high visibility, and responsibility for critical decisions.

Benefits: Gives you the opportunity to be decisive, work and learn at a fast pace, and have significant impact. Also helps you to learn to work with those higher in the organization and to handle stress.

Reshaping Your Job	Temporary Assignments	Outside the Workplace
Manage an annual organizational event with high visibility.	Manage an unexpected opportunity with high potential payoff for the business (e.g., new customer, acquisition, partner).	Manage an annual community event with high visibility.
Manage high-profile customers or business partners.		Work on a political campaign.
Represent your organization to the media.	Do a tight-deadline assignment for your boss's boss.	Run for a local office.
Write reports for your boss.	Serve on a high-visibility task force.	Chair a professional conference or convention.
	Serve on a task force working on a pressing business issue.	
	Present a proposal to senior management.	
	Write a speech for someone higher in the organization.	

Scope and Scale

Description: Managing work that is broad in scope (involving multiple functions, groups, locations, products, or services) or large in sheer size (e.g., workload, number of responsibilities).

Benefits: Gives you the opportunity to coordinate and integrate across groups, delegate to others, and create systems to monitor and track work. Also helps you to learn to feel comfortable accomplishing tasks through others.

Reshaping Your Job	Temporary Assignments	Outside the Workplace
Serve on multiple project teams simultaneously.	Take on a colleague's responsibilities during his or her absence.	Pursue the degree you've always wanted while maintaining a full-time job.
Broaden the services or products offered by your unit.	Take on a special assignment in addition to current job responsibilities.	Chair the board of a community or non-profit organization.
Take on additional responsibilities previously handled by your boss.	Serve on a team managing a large-scale project.	Serve as an officer in a regional or national professional organization.

External Pressure

Description: Managing the interface with important groups outside the organization, such as customers, vendors, partners, unions, and regulatory agencies.

Benefits: Gives you the opportunity to represent your organization, to influence and negotiate with external groups, and to build shared agendas among diverse groups. Also gives you a chance to learn to build relationships with a wide variety of people.

Reshaping Your Job	Temporary Assignments	Outside the Workplace
Add external interface roles to your job (e.g., customer or vendor negotiations, partnership relationships, government relationships).	Take calls on a customer hotline. Teach customers how to use a new product. Spend a week with a customer or vendor. Make speeches to external groups as a representative of your organization. Work at your organization's booth at a trade show. Serve as a campus recruiter. Represent the organization at a government conference. Lead a benchmarking team that visits and learns from other organizations. Create a partnership with an external organization.	Take on boundary-spanning roles for a community or professional organization (e.g., public liaison, media relationships, United Way liaison).

Influence without Authority

Description: Influencing peers, higher management, or other key people over whom you have no direct authority.

Benefits: Gives you the opportunity to work across organizational boundaries, coordinate action across the organization, and handle internal politics. Also allows you to develop a broader framework for understanding organizational issues.

Reshaping Your Job	Temporary Assignments	Outside the Workplace
Create a networking group in your organization.	Represent concerns of employees to higher management.	Become active in a professional organization.
Manage projects that require coordination across the organization.	Play an advisory role on a colleague's project.	Serve as a loaned executive to a nonprofit organization.
	Comanage a project with someone in another function.	
	Work with a colleague to get a cross-unit problem resolved.	Cochair a fundraising event for a nonprofit organization.
	Serve on a cross-functional task force or project.	
	Represent your group on a task force that prioritizes projects across groups.	Play an active role in an advocacy organization.
	Teach in a leadership development program.	
	Put together a coalition of peers who lobby the organization for a new process, system, or technology.	Teach a course at a local university or through a professional association.
	Bring a well-researched counterproposal to your boss on an issue you would like to see handled differently.	

Work across Cultures

Description: Working with people from different cultures or with institutions in other countries.

Benefits: Gives you the opportunity to become more aware of your own cultural biases, to adapt to different expectations, and to manage across distances. Also provides an opportunity to learn the traditions and values of people from different cultures.

Reshaping Your Job	Temporary Assignments	Outside the Workplace
Take on global responsibility for a product, process, or function.	Host visitors from other countries.	Serve as a host family for a foreign exchange student.
Manage a major multicountry project.	Work in a short-term assignment at your organization's office in another country (e.g., installing a new system, studying a process to bring back to your office, filling in for a short-term need, working on a special project).	Travel abroad.
Serve on a team or committee with members from other countries.		Work on a short-term service project in a foreign country.
Serve as the liaison with a business partner in another country.		Volunteer in organizations that work with immigrants or refugees.
		Take foreign language classes.

Work Group Diversity

Description: Being responsible for the work of people of both genders and different racial and ethnic backgrounds.

Benefits: Gives you the opportunity to work with diverse people, to recognize the need to overcome stereotypes and biases, and to persuade people from different backgrounds to work together. Also helps you to learn to be compassionate and sensitive to the needs of others.

Reshaping Your Job	Temporary Assignments	Outside the Workplace
Hire and develop people of different genders, ethnic groups, and races.	Lead a project team or task force with a diverse group of members.	Join special-interest networks that attract a diverse group of people.
Create internship positions in your unit to bring in diverse students.	Jointly coach an employee of a different gender, ethnic group, or race with someone of the employee's gender, ethnic group, or race serving as the other coach.	Join a community group focusing on diversity.
Train regularly in your organization's diversity program.		

4
COMPETENCY-DRIVEN ASSIGNMENTS

This chapter is designed to support development in place by targeting the development of a specific competency. If you choose this approach, look through the twenty competencies and pick the one that is most similar to the competency you want to improve. Each competency is followed by behavioral indicators. To the right is a general description of experiences that can help you develop the competency, with cross-references to the challenges in the previous chapter. Following the general description are specific examples of assignments. As in the previous chapter, the examples cover three basic ways of adding developmental assignments to your job: reshaping your job, adding a temporary assignment, and seeking a challenge outside the workplace.

Adaptability	Experiences that force you out of your routine (*Unfamiliar Responsibilities, Work across Cultures*) or force you to work with perspectives different from your own (*Influence without Authority, Work across Cultures*).
Adapts to change easily. Is open to the influence and perspectives of others.	• Take on part of a colleague's job while he/she is on temporary leave. • Focus more attention on a part of your job you've been avoiding. • Volunteer for a task in your group that would normally go to a more experienced person. • Comanage a project with someone who often represents a different perspective from your own. • Serve on a cross-functional task force or project. • Serve as a loaned executive to a nonprofit organization. • Serve as the liaison for a business partner in another country. • Volunteer in an organization that works with immigrants or refugees.

| Self-Awareness

Has accurate picture of strengths and weaknesses and of impact on others.

Seeks and uses feedback from others. | Experiences in which people more readily give you feedback because you are new to the work (*Unfamiliar Responsibilities*) or are trying to change or improve a situation (*New Directions, Inherited Problems*).

- Ask your boss to delegate one of his/her responsibilities to you and give you regular feedback on how well you are doing.
- Trade a responsibility with a colleague and then serve as each other's peer coach.
- Participate in a job rotation program, seeking feedback from each department or unit you spend time with.
- Work with colleagues to redesign a work process.
- Actively participate in the start-up of a new team.
- Take over a project that is in trouble.
- Work to improve your relationship with a difficult colleague. |

Managing Yourself	Experiences in which you can practice setting priorities, managing stress, and keeping balance amidst the pursuit of difficult goals (*Inherited Problems, Problems with Employees, High Stakes*).
Sets personal goals. Manages time well. Proactively manages own career. Handles stressful experiences with energy and resilience. Balances work priorities and personal priorities.	• Take on your unit's most dissatisfied customer or difficult supplier. • Join the board of a struggling non-profit organization. • Serve on a task force to solve a major organizational problem. • Champion a change your group has been resisting. • Manage an annual organizational event with high visibility. • Do a tight-deadline assignment for your boss's boss. • Work on a local political campaign. • Chair a professional conference.

Capacity to Learn	Experiences that add diversity (to enhance your capacity to learn) or require you to work in a completely different context (to sharpen your focus on learning).
Seeks out and reflects on new experiences. Learns from mistakes. Learns by seeking other points of view. Explores with curiosity and a sense of playfulness.	• Take up a new hobby. • Start a new group, club, or team. • Participate in a job rotation program. • Work in a short-term assignment at another office, in another region, or in another country. • Teach a course—inside or outside your organization. • Lead a benchmarking team that visits and learns from other organizations. • Become active in a professional or nonprofit organization. • Serve as a campus recruiter.

Leadership Stature Exhibits confidence, optimism, and a positive attitude.	Experiences that you are attracted to and excited about taking on (*New Directions, High Stakes, External Pressure, Work across Cultures*).
	• Join a project team that is plowing new ground in your organization.
	• Head a new initiative for a community or professional organization.
	• Seek seed money for an exploratory project you have been wanting to pursue.
	• Manage a new customer with high potential payoff for the business.
	• Represent your organization to the media.
	• Teach customers how to use a new product.
	• Pursue an advanced degree.
	• Host visitors from other countries.

Drive and Purpose	Experiences in which you play a key role in seeing that the organization achieves important outcomes (*Inherited Problems, High Stakes, Scope and Scale, External Pressure*).
Is goal directed and driven to achieve objectives. Is self-disciplined and willing to make sacrifices to contribute to the success of the organization.	• Supervise product recalls. • Supervise cost-cutting initiatives. • Regain a lost customer. • Serve on a task force working on a pressing business issue. • Manage a fund-raising event for a nonprofit organization. • Serve on a team managing a large-scale project. • Broaden the services or products offered by your unit. • Manage relationships with a government agency.

Ethics and Integrity	Experiences in which having high-trust relationships is essential (*Influence without Authority, External Pressure, Problems with Employees, Work Group Diversity*).
Tells the truth, is honest. Aligns words and actions. Consistently takes responsibility for own actions.	• Resolve a conflict with a subordinate. • Commit to handling an employee performance issue you've been avoiding. • Take calls on a customer hotline. • Take on a boundary-spanning role for a community or professional organization. • Create a partnership with an external organization. • Represent concerns of employees to higher management. • Train regularly in your organization's diversity program. • Jointly coach an employee of a different gender or ethnic group with someone of the employee's gender or ethnic group serving as the other coach.

Managing Effective Teams	Experiences managing a wide variety of teams in a wide variety of contexts.
Promotes and facilitates effective teamwork.	• Lead a cross-functional team.
	• Lead a multinational team.
	• Lead a team with members of different ethnic and racial backgrounds.
As a team leader, creates the needed processes, systems, and environment for effective team functioning.	• Lead a virtual team.
	• Lead a team fixing problems.
	• Lead a team coordinating the introduction of new systems.
	• Lead a team exploring new opportunities.
	• Lead a short-term task-focused team.
	• Lead a long-term project team.
	• Lead a standing committee.
	• Lead a team of volunteers.

Building and Maintaining Relationships	Experiences in which you are working with others to create change (*New Directions, Inherited Problems*) or are working across boundaries (*Influence without Authority, External Pressure*).
Develops cooperative and positive relationships. Manages conflict effectively. Shows genuine interest in and empathy toward others.	• Be responsible for a new project or new process in your group. • Head a new initiative in a community or professional organization. • Be trained as a volunteer mediator. • Manage a continuous quality improvement process in your group. • Work with a colleague to get a cross-unit problem solved. • Manage projects that require coordination across the organization. • Create a networking group in your organization. • Represent your organization at a government conference.

Valuing Diversity and Difference	Experiences that expose you to the value of diversity and difference (*Work across Cultures, Work Group Diversity*).
Values and leverages perspectives from different people and cultures. Works effectively with people who differ in race, gender, culture, age, or background. Adapts behavior to fit cultural expectations.	• Create internship positions in your group to bring in diverse students. • Lead a project team or task force with a diverse group of members. • Join special-interest networks that attract a diverse group of people. • Train regularly in your organization's diversity program. • Manage a major multicountry project. • Take on global responsibility for a product, process, or function. • Serve as a host family for a foreign exchange student. • Work on a short-term service project in a foreign country.

Developing Others	Experiences in which you must motivate and develop employees to be successful (*New Directions, Inherited Problems, Problems with Employees, Work Group Diversity*).
Provides effective feedback, coaching, and support for development of others.	• Lead the start-up of a new team.
	• Delegate one of your job responsibilities to a direct report.
Selects talented and committed employees.	• Manage the training of new employees in your group.
Effectively delegates responsibilities.	• Hire and develop an employee who shows promise but doesn't have the needed experience for the job.
Recognizes and rewards the contributions of others.	• Work to retain a valued employee who is thinking about leaving the organization.
	• Fire an employee who has not met performance standards despite coaching and support.
Acts decisively and with fairness in dealing with problem employees.	• Coach a sports team.
	• Hire and develop people of different gender, ethnic groups, and races.

Communicating Effectively	Experiences that allow you to practice your communication skills with different audiences.
Expresses ideas clearly and concisely.	• Participate in a speaker's bureau.
	• Train in one of your organization's employee development programs.
Communicates in ways that inspire enthusiasm.	• Make a presentation to top management.
	• Write a speech for someone higher in the organization.
Disseminates information about decisions, plans, and activities.	• Serve as a subject matter expert in media interviews.
	• Make speeches to external groups as a representative of your organization.
	• Write reports for your boss.
Listens carefully and is open to the input of others.	• Write for your organization's internal newsletter.

Managing Change	Experiences in which you are creating new directions or fixing problems (*New Directions, Inherited Problems*).
Uses effective strategies to facilitate organization change initiatives.	• Be responsible for a new project or new process in your group.
	• Volunteer your work group as a test site for a new organizational system or process.
Recognizes the emotional impact of change.	• Join a project team opening a new market.
	• Join a project team installing new systems.
	• Represent your group on a task force making changes in organizational policies.
	• Lead a task force to fix a problem (e.g., correct a quality problem, redesign a flawed system, streamline a process).
	• Work with your direct reports as a group to reorganize their work responsibilities to better fit with organizational priorities.
	• Help facilitate the merger of two community or nonprofit organizations.

Solving Problems and Making Decisions	Experiences that provide opportunities to work on ill-defined or recurring problems, or to make decisions that require broad input from across the organization or decisions that groups have avoided addressing.
Synthesizes and creates order out of large quantities of information.	• Ask your group to give you one new problem a year to solve.
Pays attention to weak signals, the periphery, and "white spaces" between groups.	• Lead a quality improvement initiative in a nonprofit or professional organization. • Work with a colleague to get a cross-unit problem solved.
Is insightful and asks good questions.	• Represent your group on a task force that prioritizes projects across groups. • Improve the metrics used to assess your group's effectiveness.
Makes timely decisions—not too quick or too slow—and bases them on adequate information.	• Investigate and make a decision about an outsourcing option. • Investigate and make a decision about a potential acquisition. • Investigate and make a decision about whether to continue resourcing a project that continues to underperform.
Works to understand the trade-offs and the short- and long-term implications of various decision options.	

Managing Politics and Influencing Others	Experiences in which you are working across organizational boundaries or influencing without hierarchical power (*External Pressure, Scope and Scale, Influence without Authority*) or engaged in high-visibility work (*High Stakes*).
Understands and negotiates across political boundaries.	• Manage an annual organizational event with high visibility.
	• Play a key role in a community fund-raising event.
Effectively influences others in a variety of situations.	• Take on a boundary-spanning responsibility previously handled by your boss.
Gets action and commitment by forging relationships inside and outside the organization.	• Put together a coalition of peers who lobby the organization for a new process, system, or technology.
	• Work on a project that requires coordination across the organization.
	• Bring a well-researched counterproposal to your boss on an issue you would like to see him/her handle differently.
	• Work with the manager of a unit your group often has conflict with to create a better working partnership.

Taking Risks and Innovating	Experiences in which you and others are bringing fresh perspective to a situation or need to find new solutions to problems.
Is willing to take a stand when others disagree, to go against the status quo.	• Work on a new product development team.
	• Work on a task force tackling a new business issue.
Generates new ideas and innovative solutions.	• Spend time with customers and find out what they think their needs will be in the future.
Finds and seizes new opportunities.	• Go on an adventure (e.g., travel somewhere you haven't been, go to events you never attend, seek out people you don't normally meet).
	• Ask your team to give you one new problem a year to solve.
	• Work on a problem by doing quick experiments and trials.
	• Advocate for a social or environmental cause.
	• Advocate for an idea that you feel strongly about but that is unpopular with some of your peers.

Setting Vision and Strategy	Experiences that allow you to think about possible futures and craft strategies for aligning people and systems to achieve long-term objectives.
Creates a common vision in complex situations. Translates vision and long-term objectives into realistic business strategy.	• Work on a strategic plan for your unit. • Work on a strategic plan for a community or professional organization. • Develop five-year business scenarios for your unit. • Develop processes for tracking progress toward long-term goals. • Join a project team that is plowing new ground in your organization. • Study and report on the impact of emerging technologies on your work. • Take a temporary assignment in the strategic planning group. • Take a temporary assignment in new product development.

Managing the Work	Experiences that draw on managerial knowledge and expertise.
Quickly obtains necessary technical and business knowledge for managing one's responsibilities. Organizes, prioritizes, and aligns work to achieve important objectives.	• Manage a project. • Coach a new project manager. • Take over the project manager role from someone who left suddenly. • Organize a short-timeframe event, like the annual United Way campaign. • Serve as a loaned executive to a nonprofit organization. • Engage your direct reports in a goal alignment exercise. • Take a project in chaos and get it back on track. • Volunteer to teach someone else something you don't know well.

Business Skills and Knowledge	Experiences that expose you to parts of the business you are less familiar with (*Unfamiliar Responsibilities*).
Has broad range of business knowledge and skills (e.g., customer relations, marketing, sales, financial management, human resources, international business).	• Trade a responsibility with a colleague. • Take on part of a colleague's job while he/she is on temporary leave. • Represent your group on a task force or committee doing work you know little about. • Serve on cross-functional project teams. • Design your own job rotation program: spend four to six weeks in three other units that interface with your own unit. • When your team has a missing business skill, ask an internal expert to serve as the team's advisor and coach. • Design and deliver a workshop to help colleagues learn more about a "hot" topic in another function. • Volunteer for a committee outside your area of expertise (e.g., the finance committee, the marketing committee) in a community or professional organization.

Understanding and Navigating the Organization	Experiences in which you must operate within broader strategic initiatives, competing priorities, and a network of relationships.
Makes decisions and takes action consistent with the strategic direction of the organization.	• Take a temporary assignment in another part of the business to better understand its priorities.
	• Facilitate a quarterly review of your group's actions and assess its alignment with strategic goals (invite your boss to observe).
Deals effectively with the multiple priorities of the organization.	• Work on a Total Quality Management or process-reengineering project that crosses functional or business unit boundaries.
	• Serve on the board of a nonprofit organization.
Establishes collaborative relationships and alliances throughout the organization.	• Serve on multiple project teams simultaneously.
	• Ask your group to generate a new idea they want to implement; work to move that idea through the organization and get the necessary buy-in from others.
	• Work with a colleague in another function (whom you often disagree with) on a project proposal.

APPENDIX A: RESOURCES

Byham, W. C., Smith, A. B., & Paese, M. J. (2002). *Grow your own leaders: How to identify, develop, and retain leadership talent.* New York: Prentice Hall.

Dalton, M. A. (1998). *Becoming a more versatile learner.* Greensboro, NC: Center for Creative Leadership.

Lombardo, M. M., & Eichinger, R. W. (1989). *Eighty-eight assignments for development in place.* Greensboro, NC: Center for Creative Leadership.

Lombardo, M. M., & Eichinger, R. W. (2000). *For your improvement: A development and coaching guide* (3rd ed.). Minneapolis, MN: Lominger.

McCall, M. W., Jr., & Hollenbeck, G. P. (2002). *Developing global executives: The lessons of international experience.* Boston: Harvard Business School Press.

McCall, M. W., Jr., Lombardo, M. M., & Morrison, A. M. (1988). *The lessons of experience: How successful executives develop on the job.* San Francisco: New Lexington Press.

McCauley, C. D., & Martineau, J. (1998). *Reaching your development goals.* Greensboro, NC: Center for Creative Leadership.

McCauley, C. D., Ohlott, P. O., & Ruderman, M. N. (1999). *Job challenge profile facilitator's guide: Learning from work experience.* San Francisco: Jossey-Bass.

Ohlott, P. O. (2004). Job assignments. In C. D. McCauley & E. Van Velsor (Eds.), *The Center for Creative Leadership handbook of leadership development* (2nd ed., pp. 151-182). San Francisco: Jossey-Bass.

Ruderman, M. N., & Ohlott, P. O. (2000). *Learning from life: Turning life's lessons into leadership experiences.* Greensboro, NC: Center for Creative Leadership.

APPENDIX B: DEVELOPMENTAL ASSIGNMENT PLAN TEMPLATE

Developmental Assignment Plan
Developmental Assignment:
Time Frame:
Target of Development:
Skills, Behaviors, Actions to Practice: •   •   •
Resources to Access: •   •   •
Relationships to Put in Place: •   •   •
Other Strategies: •   •   •

APPENDIX C: 360 BY DESIGN CROSS-REFERENCES

If you want to target the development of specific competencies as a result of receiving feedback from 360 by Design, these cross-references will direct you to appropriate assignments based on that feedback. These are the specific competencies for 360 by Design, along with page numbers for related assignments.

LEADING OTHERS

Managing Effective Teams

Building and Maintaining Relationships

Valuing Diversity and Difference

Developing Others

LEADING THE ORGANIZATION

Understanding and Navigating the Organization

Problems That Can Stall a Career

LEADING YOURSELF

Adaptability

Self-Awareness

Managing Yourself

Capacity to Learn

APPENDIX D: EXECUTIVE DIMENSIONS CROSS-REFERENCES

If you want to target the development of specific competencies as a result of receiving feedback from Executive Dimensions, these cross-references will direct you to appropriate assignments based on that feedback. These are the specific competencies for Executive Dimensions, along with page numbers for related assignments.

Leading the Business

Leading Others

Leading by Personal Example

APPENDIX E: BENCHMARKS CROSS-REFERENCES

If you want to target the development of specific competencies as a result of receiving feedback from Benchmarks, these cross-references will direct you to appropriate assignments based on that feedback. These are the specific competencies for Benchmarks, along with page numbers for related assignments.

Meeting Job Challenges

Resourcefulness, 45
Doing whatever it takes, 37
Being a quick study, 49
Decisiveness, 45

Respecting Self and Others

Building and mending relationships, 40
Compassion and sensitivity, 40
Straightforwardness and composure, 34
Balance between personal life and work, 34
Self-awareness, 33
Putting people at ease, 40
Differences matter, 41
Career management, 34

Leading People

Leading employees, 42
Confronting problem employees, 42
Participative management, 43
Change management, 44

APPENDIX F: PROSPECTOR CROSS-REFERENCES

If you want to target the development of specific competencies as a result of receiving feedback from Prospector, these cross-references will direct you to appropriate assignments based on that feedback. These are the specific competencies for Prospector, along with page numbers for related assignments.

Learning to Learn

Seeks opportunities to learn, 35
Seeks and uses feedback, 33
Learns from mistakes, 35
Open to criticism, 33

Learning to Lead

Committed to making a difference, 37
Insightful, sees things from new angles, 45
Has the courage to take risks, 47
Brings out the best in people, 39
Acts with integrity, 38
Seeks broad business knowledge, 49
Adapts to cultural differences, 41

APPENDIX G: SKILLSCOPE CROSS-REFERENCES

If you want to target the development of specific competencies as a result of receiving feedback from Skillscope, these cross-references will direct you to appropriate assignments based on that feedback. These are the specific competencies for Skillscope, along with page numbers for related assignments.

Information Skills

Getting and making sense of information, 45
Communicating information and ideas, 43

Decision Making

Taking action, making decisions, 45
Risk taking and innovation, 47
Administrative, organizational ability, 49
Managing conflict and negotiation, 40

Interpersonal Skills

Relationships, 40
Selecting, developing people, 42
Influencing, leadership, power, 46
Openness to influence and flexibility, 32

Personal Resources

Knowledge of job and business, 49
Energy, drive, ambition, 37

Effective Use of Self

Ordering Information

To get more information, to order other CCL Press publications, or to find out about bulk-order discounts, please contact us by phone at 336-545-2810 or visit our online bookstore at **www.ccl.org/publications**.